# California Missions
## Coloring Book

### DAVID RICKMAN

DOVER PUBLICATIONS, INC., New York

*California Missions Coloring Book* is a new work, first published by Dover Publications, Inc., in 1992.

*International Standard Book Number*

*ISBN-13: 978-0-486-27346-4*
*ISBN-10: 0-486-27346-6*

Manufactured in the United States by LSC Communications
27346614    2020
www.doverpublications.com

*To my dear friend Michael Tucker,*
*who has always helped me put*
*things into perspective*

# ACKNOWLEDGMENTS

I would like to thank some of those who were instrumental in inspiring and assisting me to complete this book. Above all, to my dear wife, Deborah Kraak, whose love and belief in me are so sustaining, I give thanks. Also, I am grateful to my parents, who introduced me to the missions as a child and who have so wanted this book. I am also indebted to my friends Ed Vebell and Eric von Schmidt, artists and historians. For their generosity to me I thank Ron Dupuy, Joe McCummins and the volunteers at La Purísima State Historic Park, Edna Kimbro, David Debs of the Los Angeles County Museum of Natural History, Richard Clark of the California Department of Parks and Recreation, and Heidi Mattson.

# INTRODUCTION

*Junípero Serra, the leader of the Franciscan monks, . . . established a chain of missions along the California coast, and for fifty years created there the idyllic pastoral life, now seen only in the poet's dream of Arcadia.*
— From *West of the Rocky Mountains*, edited by John Muir, 1888

The romance of the California missions has been part of America's mythology since the middle of the last century. By then, California was part of the United States and the era of the missions was a rapidly fading memory for those who had been witnesses to it. Yet the neglected ruins of the missions had a fascination for the newly arrived Americans, and the legend they inspired of a golden age remains even today. But what was the reality behind the legend?

A visitor to the California missions seeking to understand what life was like there in their heyday might be misled by their present-day appearance. Take Mission Santa Bárbara for example. Surrounded by an exclusive residential community, the mission's buildings and grounds are just too pristine, too well-landscaped to allow us to believe that anyone ever lived there at all. And if they once did, it is now so peaceful and pretty that it is hard to shake those visions of kindly padres and humble Indians inspired by such fictions as *Ramona* and the adventures of Zorro. Not until the visitor steps into the little graveyard beside the church is he or she confronted by a clue to the reality of those days. Here is the resting place of four thousand Native Americans, former neophytes of the mission. *Four thousand*. Santa Bárbara existed as a mission for less than fifty years. In that time it baptized some five and a half thousand Indians and buried three quarters of them.

The record is much the same throughout the mission chain, proving as nothing else can that life here was anything but idyllic for the Indians. Does that mean, then, that the missions were an absolute evil, which only aided in the destruction of those they claimed to protect? The answer is not a simple one.

Indians were an economic necessity to Spain. Unlike other New World colonial powers, such as France and England, Spain sent comparatively few of her citizens to colonize America, preferring instead to harness the labor of the Indians to serve a small white elite. Not all Spaniards were grandees, of course. Many served as soldiers, craftsmen, merchants or priests, but very few as common laborers.

A system of converting Indians into a useful, and docile, peasant class began to develop as Spain pushed its empire northward from Mexico. The army and the church became partners in this task. The padres' job was to persuade the Indians to accept Christianity and settlement in the socialist community of the mission. Classed as *neófitos*, neophytes, the Indian converts at the mission received instruction in the Catholic faith. Men learned to be farm and ranch hands, or to master such crafts as blacksmithing and carpentry. Women learned to become good housewives and mothers, according to Spanish notions, and might perhaps acquire such crafts as weaving and candlemaking.

At first these skills were to help support the mission, but once the "wild" Indians of a region had been transformed and settled into their villages as peasants, then, in theory, the mission lands and property would be divided among the Indians, and the mission would become just a parish church. This evolution was supposed to take about ten years. Meanwhile, it was the army's job to explore and subdue the new lands, guard the missions and round up runaways, for once the Indian accepted conversion, there was no going back to the wild.

The final stage of this process involved the third wing of conquest, the *pobladores*, the colonists, the townsmen. These mostly Spanish settlers were expected to move into the areas subdued by soldiers and priests and become the necessary middle class and elite of the province.

It was a remarkably thorough system, which looked wonderful on paper. If it never worked as perfectly in actual practice, it worked well enough. By the eighteenth century, Spain's "internal provinces" of Texas, New Mexico and Arizona were held together by a network of missions, presidios (forts) and pueblos (towns). The only problem was that these provinces, lacking the great mineral wealth of Mexico, were always worth more as a buffer zone against Indian raiders and the encroachment of foreign empires than for what they might contribute to the royal treasuries. Though claiming a far greater portion of the West, Spain had no immediate plans to explore, much less colonize, any more territory.

California was ignored by Spain for more than two hundred years after her explorers first landed there in 1542. Then word of Russian activities in Alaska and English explorations in the Pacific Ocean alerted the Spanish Empire to the need to secure California through settlements. A combined naval and land force was sent to bring the first settlers to the port of San Diego in 1769. The two ships that arrived carried most of the supplies as well as soldiers, artisans and priests. Traveling overland came a party of soldiers, Indians and muleteers, as well as the now legendary Padre Junípero Serra, who commanded the missionary arm of the expedition.

Serra was a zealous leader. By the time of his death, in 1784, nine missions had been founded against great odds in a chain stretching from San Diego to San Francisco Bay. In the coming years, a total of twenty-one would be established, the last in 1823.

It must be acknowledged that the Franciscan friars who came to California, especially those first pioneers, were idealists. They dedicated their lives to a task that brought mostly hard work, periods of scarcity, isolation from their countrymen and sometimes physical danger, without the possibility of either fame or financial reward at the end of it all. Yet the question that was asked even by some of their contemporaries, and that still remains to be answered, is: what good did they do?

In an era in which every soldier expected a portion of the land and Indians of a conquered territory as their just reward, the missions represented a more humane alternative. Since California was to be conquered and settled by Spain, the padres probably thought that the Indians should be grateful to the missions, whose stated purpose was to preserve their lives and property rights. Then, too, in the view of the padres, they had saved the Indians' souls, which was something even more valuable.

But from the perspective of the California Indians, the arrival of the Spanish must have been nothing less than disastrous. It meant the death of untold thousands through new diseases, and the destruction of the environment they knew by the introduction of farming and of vast herds of grazing animals. It meant, too, the end of a way of life that was of the Native Californians' own making. In its place was imposed a regimen of continuous toil, punctuated by corporal punishment for those who broke the rules. At its best, the treatment of the neophytes was paternalistic; they were treated as children for as long as they lived.

From the first, at least some of the Native Californians were unwilling to accept missionization without a struggle. At San Diego in 1769, and again several years later, uprisings of the Indians ended with loss of life on both sides, but were decided by the Spaniards' firearms. The largest revolt in the mission chain took place in 1824 and involved the neophytes of Santa Inés, Santa Bárbara and La Purísima. Triggered by the beating of a neophyte by soldiers, this rebellion would see mission buildings in the hands of neophytes armed with Spanish weapons. But it, like the other rebellions, would end in defeat for the Indians. Many of the rebels escaped into the wilderness in which, throughout the mission era, so many had sought safety.

Disastrous as the mission era was for the California Indians, what followed certainly proved no better. The expected ten years required to transform the Indians into a free peasant class was well past when, in 1833, the order for the missions to secularize, to cease operations, arrived in the by then Mexican province of California. The lands and property of the missions were distributed to the Indians, but most passed quickly into the hands of certain Hispanic citizens who took advantage of the Indians' naïveté about private property. Many of the newly liberated neophytes found themselves working for food and shelter at ranchos built on what should have been their land. Others haunted the pueblos or else withdrew to build their villages on unwanted land, returning as much as possible to the old life. In American times they would lose their claim to even these scraps of land and be forced to settle on reservations.

As for the missions themselves, the years following secularization saw most of them fall steadily into ruin, to await the day when a new generation and a new culture would restore them as monuments to an earlier and what was imagined to be a golden era.

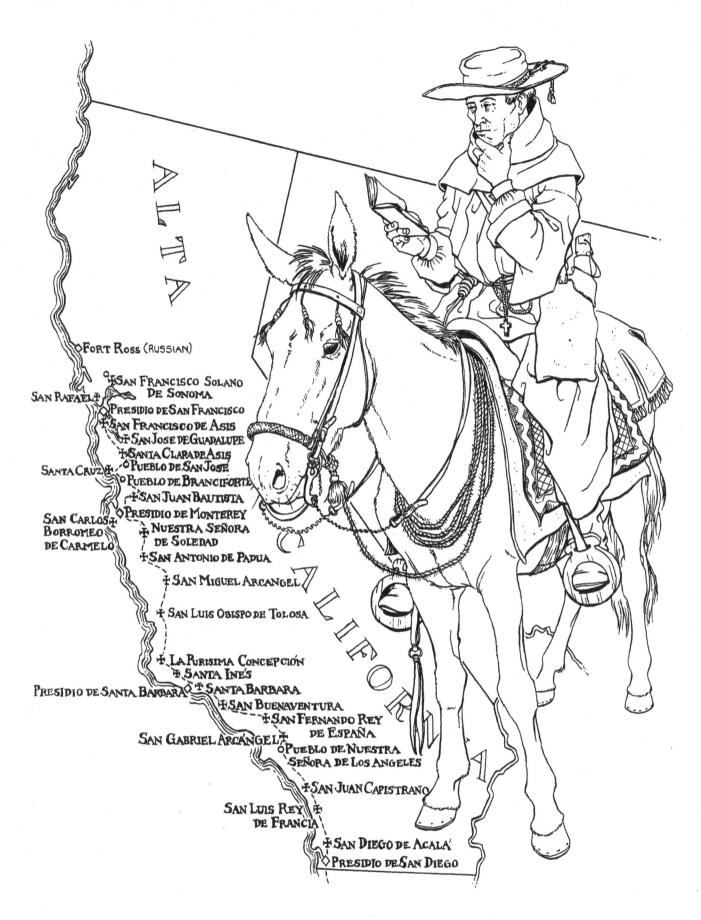

ALTA

CALIFORNIA

FORT ROSS (RUSSIAN)

SAN FRANCISCO SOLANO
DE SONOMA
SAN RAFAEL
PRESIDIO DE SAN FRANCISCO
SAN FRANCISCO DE ASIS
SAN JOSE DE GUADALUPE
SANTA CLARA DE ASIS
SANTA CRUZ
PUEBLO DE SAN JOSE
PUEBLO DE BRANCIFORTE
SAN JUAN BAUTISTA
PRESIDIO DE MONTEREY
SAN CARLOS
BORROMEO
DE CARMELO
NUESTRA SEÑORA
DE SOLEDAD
SAN ANTONIO DE PADUA
SAN MIGUEL ARCANGEL
SAN LUIS OBISPO DE TOLOSA
LA PURISIMA CONCEPCIÓN
SANTA INES
PRESIDIO DE SANTA BARBARA
SANTA BARBARA
SAN BUENAVENTURA
SAN FERNANDO REY
DE ESPAÑA
SAN GABRIEL ARCANGEL
PUEBLO DE NUESTRA
SEÑORA DE LOS ANGELES
SAN JUAN CAPISTRANO
SAN LUIS REY
DE FRANCIA
SAN DIEGO DE ACALÁ
PRESIDIO DE SAN DIEGO

The Franciscan missions of California were founded with
the purpose of Christianizing the native peoples and inte-
grating them into the culture of the Spaniards who sought
to rule them. In the fifty-four years following the arrival of
the first Spaniards in San Diego in 1769, twenty-one
missions grew up along the coast of California. From San
Diego to Sonoma the Camino Real, the King's Highway,
connected mission, presidio (fort) and pueblo (town).

The natives of California already had religions of their own before the arrival of the missionaries. Their ancient beliefs permeated every aspect of daily life and included a deep respect for the world of nature. This shaman or holy man from an area near Santa Barbara wears feathered ceremonial clothing. The feather-topped post was revered as a symbol of a spirit his people honored.

The natives of California belonged to a large number of separate groups speaking a wide variety of languages. They were politically disunited and at a very simple economic level. Mostly peaceable, they lived on what they hunted and gathered. Though they greeted the Spaniards hospitably, happily accepted their gifts and were often willing to undergo baptism and relocation to the missions, nothing could have prepared these peoples for the fundamental changes they were about to experience.

With their conversion, the Native Californians were expected to accept the rule of the Franciscans over their daily lives and to take up permanent residence at a mission. The Spanish generally did not use force to convert the Native Californians, but they did use it to ensure that the new converts, or neophytes, remained. Spanish cavalry, still armed and armored much like medieval knights, regularly tracked down those neophytes who sought to flee the missions and return to their old ways.

At the founding of each mission, a wooden cross was raised and blessed, after which the building of shelter could begin. The first structures were simple *jacales*, or huts, made of upright posts plastered with mud and thatched with reeds. In coming years, once the padres could teach the neophytes the necessary skills, there would follow more permanent buildings of adobe and even stone.

10

The Spaniards found the peoples of California living in relative abundance on the native plants and animals. Intending to transform the Indians into a useful peasant class, the padres instructed them in an agriculture not much advanced beyond that of medieval Europe. For example, the plough was roughly shaped from a tree branch and its tip shod with iron, while the yoke was tied to the oxen's horns.

Girls at the missions, from the age of eight until they were married, were confined along with widows in the *monjerio* (women's quarters). This was their dormitory, where they were locked in at night and where they took their meals. It was here, also, that they were given their catechism. Instructed in homemaking by their *maestras*, or teacher/mistresses, they were not allowed out of the *monjerio* until their allotted tasks were completed. They were punished for disobedience.

The purpose of the missions was not only to convert the Native Californians to Catholic Christianity, but to transform them into a useful peasant class for the colony. Therefore the neophytes were taught the crafts of home and farm according to European notions. Women were schooled in such tasks as spinning and weaving. Blankets and cloth produced in mission workshops not only served the missions, but helped to supply the presidios and pueblos as well.

Capistrano

La Soledad

San Diego

Santa Cruz

San Antonio

S. Luis Obispo

Sta. Bárbara

Solano

San Rafael

From the first small bands of livestock brought to California by the early settlers, the mission herds multiplied bewilderingly until, by 1832, the cattle alone totaled more than 150,000. An important part of the missions' income came from the sale of cattle hides and tallow to foreign traders, who then sold them to leather and soap manufacturers. To keep track of such numbers, each mission had its own mark, which was burned onto the calves in the

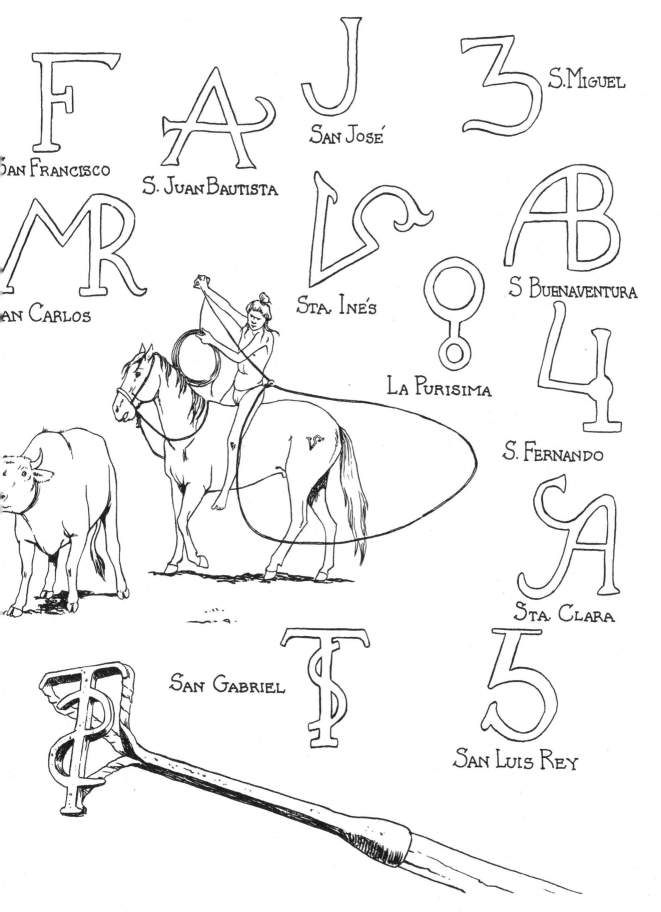

F
San Francisco

A
S. Juan Bautista

J
San José

3
S. Miguel

M R
San Carlos

S
Sta. Inés

O
La Purisima

A B
S Buenaventura

4
S. Fernando

A
Sta. Clara

San Gabriel

T
San Luis Rey

5

spring with the *fierro*, or branding-iron. Neophytes who worked as *vaqueros* (cowboys) had greater status than common herdsmen because they had mastered a much-needed skill. Trained men were called *vaqueros con sillas*, because they rode on saddles. They were entitled to wear the clothing of a Spaniard.

The California Indians had practiced the art of painting long before the Spaniards arrived, so the decorations of the mission churches and other buildings reflect the meeting of the two cultures. With hand-ground pigments, Spanish and native craftsmen executed their designs on whitewashed walls, both inside and out. Cats were valued as mousers and at several missions holes have been found cut into the doors for their convenience.

**San Diego de Alcalá, founded 1769.** Named for a 15th-century Franciscan saint, this was the first mission established in California. As with many of the missions, San Diego was built, moved, destroyed and rebuilt more than once in its history. The church on today's site was rebuilt following an Indian uprising in 1775, destroyed by an earthquake in 1803 and enlarged ten years later. At one point the diagonal walls of the porch were enclosed and roofed over.

**San Carlos Borromeo de Carmelo, founded 1770.** A year after the founding of San Diego, Father Junípero Serra established a mission in northern California. Situated near the provincial capital, Monterey, Mission San Carlos served for more than thirty years as the head of the missions chain. The present church, dedicated in 1797, was built under the direction of a master mason brought from Mexico.

**San Antonio de Padua, founded 1771.** Located in relative isolation in hilly country southeast of Monterey, San Antonio looks today much as it did in mission times. This prosperous mission was once home to some 1,300 Indians who labored at various crafts and in the orchards and fields. More than 17,000 head of livestock, including cattle, horses and sheep, grazed on San Antonio's seemingly boundless pastures.

**San Gabriel Arcángel, founded 1771.** Located some nine miles away from what later became the pueblo of Los Angeles, San Gabriel was known as the "Queen of the

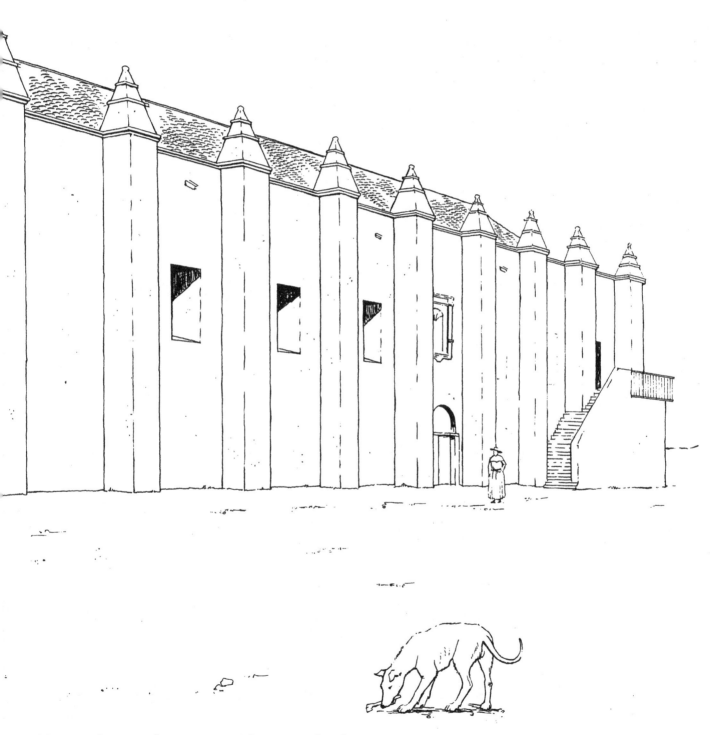

Missions," because of its prosperity. The present church
was started in 1779 and is unusual because its main entrance is on the side rather than at one end.

**San Luis Obispo de Tolosa, founded 1772.** The adobe church now found at the site was begun in 1792. Its simple rectangular shape was elaborated only by the addition of a belfry-vestibule in front of the main entrance and a colonnade outside the priests' quarters. In addition to other clocks, all the missions boasted a sundial. San Luis Obispo's was mounted prominently on a column.

**San Francisco de Asís (Mission Dolores), founded
1776.** Named for Saint Francis of Assisi, this mission
gained its other name from having been established on the
banks of a creek named for Our Lady of Sorrows (*Nuestra
Señora de los Dolores*). Located in the heart of what is
today the city of San Francisco, the church continues to be
called Mission Dolores to this day. The present structure
replaced the original wooden one in 1791. The facade is
depicted here as it appeared in 1816.

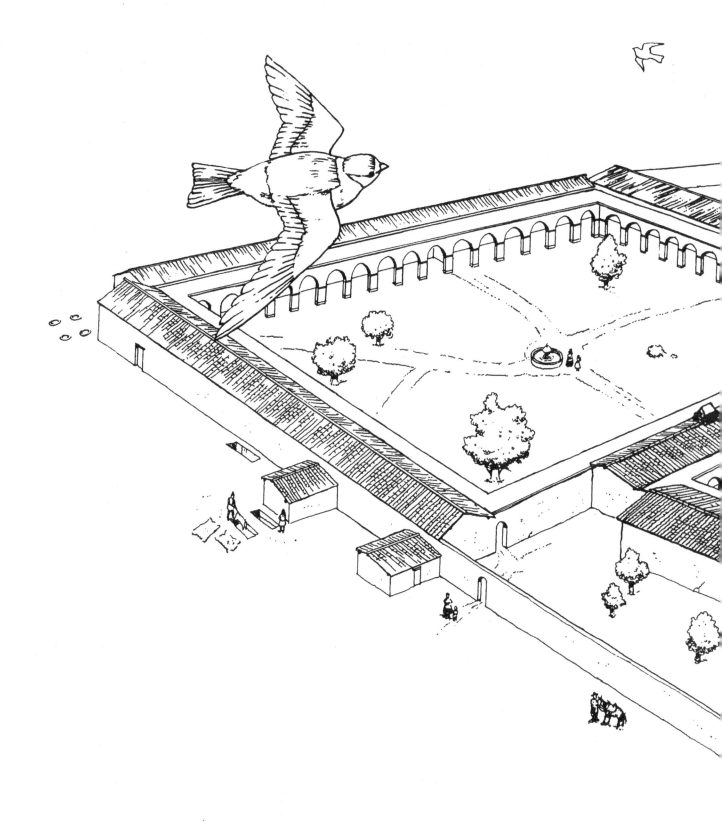

**San Juan Capistrano, founded 1775–1776.** Originally dedicated in 1775, the site was reestablished a year later following an Indian uprising in San Diego. After that the mission's enterprises flourished. The quadrangle of buildings housed workplaces for weavers, carpenters, blacksmiths and makers of hats, shoes, saddlery, soap and candles. There were storehouses for grain, olive oil, wine, hides and other goods. From 1796 to 1806 the Indian

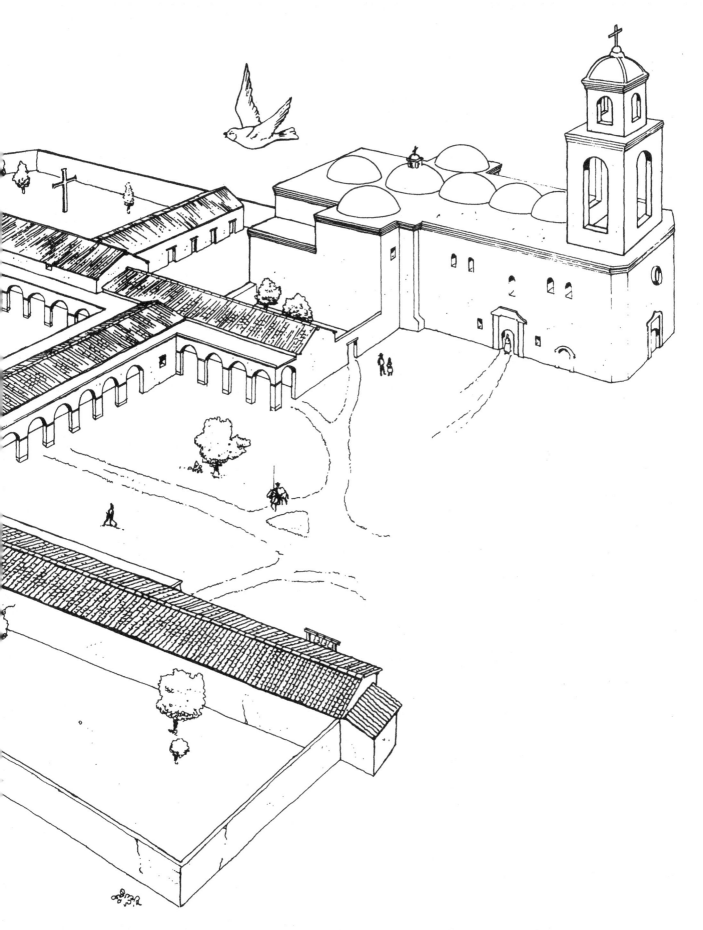

neophytes, guided by a Mexican mason, labored to build the largest church in all the missions and crowned it with a belltower 120 feet tall. In 1812, just six years after completion, the church was almost totally destroyed by an earth-quake. The mission recovered and services were held in the original church. The return of the cliff swallows from each year's migration is celebrated in legend.

**Santa Clara de Asís, founded 1777.** The church of Santa Clara was rebuilt several times during its history; the last was built in 1825 and replaced in 1929. Its charmingly painted original exterior decoration was not uncommon on other mission churches, and is known from prints and early photographs. On Sundays, people from the neighboring pueblo of San José would travel down a tree-lined avenue to the mission church to hear Mass. This unpaved avenue, called the Alameda, had been planted with willows by order of the padres, to make the journey more pleasant. In the American period the mission became the foundation for a university run by the Jesuits.

**San Buenaventura, founded 1782.** Named for a medieval Italian saint and scholar, this was the last mission established in California by Father Junípero Serra, who died some two years after its founding. Here, as elsewhere in the mission chain, the buildings suffered from periodic earthquakes. The worst came in 1812, after which the damaged church was rebuilt with a massive reinforcing buttress.

**Santa Bárbara Virgen y Mártir, founded 1786.** Named for the legendary Christian girl whose pagan father imprisoned her in a tower and later beheaded her, only to be himself struck by lightning, Santa Barbara is the only mission with matching belltowers. This fourth and present church was completed in 1820, with later changes. The carved-stone fountain dates from 1808. The title of "Queen of the Missions" has also been given to Santa Barbara.

The missions in the vicinity of the Santa Barbara Channel were established to convert the populous Chumash tribes. The coastal Chumash were noted for their canoes made from planks of redwood caulked with pitch. So impressed were the Spaniards by these canoes, with which the natives crossed even open ocean to reach the Channel Islands, that they often made use of them and their crews to carry messages and ferry passengers.

**La Purísima Concepción de María Santísima, founded 1787.** So named because of its establishment on the feast day of the Immaculate Conception, the original settlement was destroyed by earthquakes in 1812. A few miles away the padres began a new mission, which was completed in 1818. Then, in 1824, La Purísima was held for almost a month by the Indians, in an unsuccessful uprising. Located in a quiet valley, the restored mission appears today very much as it must have when presidial soldiers carried the mail along the Camino Real in a system similar to the later Pony Express.

Skilled craftsmen were always in demand in California. From time to time blacksmiths, weavers, carpenters and other master workmen were specially recruited from Mexico, paid by government contract and expected to train Indian neophytes in their particular craft. Though iron had to be imported and was never plentiful in California, there was a blacksmith shop at almost every mission. The shop illustrated here is based on one excavated and restored at Mission La Purísima.

**Santa Cruz, founded 1791.** Most of the mission churches were built in the basilican form, with a simple rectangular sanctuary. Seen here as it looked in 1811, the church at Santa Cruz (Holy Cross) was typical. The foundation and facade were of stone. Wooden tie beams helped to support both the adobe walls and the ridgepole, while the roof was finished with terra-cotta tiles. In later years wooden floors would replace dirt, and a portico and bell-tower were added, as were thick buttresses to shore up earthquake damage. Nevertheless, by 1857 the church was mostly destroyed by earthquakes and neglect.

The architecture of the California missions, whether for a church or secular building, was based on the same basic forms and techniques. A row of recently restored adobes at Mission Santa Cruz, for example, are typical of the workshops and dwellings of neophyte families found at the rest of the missions. Completed in 1824, these buildings have foundations of rough stones and mortar some 33 inches thick, topped by walls of bricks made of adobe mud and plastered with more mud. Each apartment had a floor of terra-cotta tiles and a loft, while the roof was finished with a layer of tule (bulrush) mats and mud covered with curved tiles. The smoke from the open hearth was expected to find its own way out.

**Nuestra Señora de la Soledad, founded 1791.** An era came to an end in 1834, when the missions were secularized. Intended by the Spanish government as a temporary stage in the transformation of the Indians into free peasants, the Mexican government deemed the job complete and shut the missions down. Long before that, the mission named for Our Lady of Solitude was failing.

Founded in 1791 in an isolated valley, the settlement was plagued by repeated floods. In the few decades of its existence, almost thirty missionaries came and left, many suffering from rheumatism. An American visitor, viewing the ruins in 1849, wrote, "A more desolate place cannot well be imagined."

**San José de Guadalupe, founded 1797.** Nestled in the hills overlooking San Francisco Bay, Mission San José was established to serve the *contra costa* (eastern) side of the bay. This mission was for many years headed by the talented Father Narciso Durán, who organized a noteworthy thirty-piece band from among the neophytes, with instruments ordered from Mexico and uniforms purchased from a French ship.

**San Juan Bautista, founded 1797.** Located on the Camino Real, the main north–south route, San Juan Bautista early on attracted civilian settlers, who established a small town around the mission. On Sundays the self-styled *gente de razón* ("people of reason," to distinguish themselves from the Indians) would dress in their finest clothing and ride to Mass. The town and mission, though not unchanged by passing years, remain today in much the same relationship as they enjoyed more than a century and a half ago.

**San Miguel Arcángel, founded 1797.** In 1806, much of San Miguel, both buildings and contents, was consumed by flames. The new church was begun in 1816, its tile roof intended in part to protect it from fire. After that, the mission flourished. In the foreground of the illustration is one of the roughly built *carretas*, the only wheeled vehicles in use in California in mission times. Drawn by oxen, its wheels greased with tallow, a *carreta* was slow-moving but reliable.

The severe exterior of the church at San Miguel belies its splendid interior. Created in 1820 by Indian artists under the direction of Estevan Munras, the decorations are still to be seen today. The walls are bright with carved and painted designs adapted from books found in the mission library. Over the statue of Saint Michael the artists placed the all-seeing eye of God, while suspended from the sounding board of the pulpit is a small wooden dove, symbolizing the inspiration of the Holy Spirit.

**San Fernando Rey de España, founded 1797.** When the earthquake of 1812 destroyed much of the third, 1806, church of San Fernando (the one in the illustration), it was rebuilt with additional beams and with brick buttressing. Except for this, the history of San Fernando during the mission era is one of relative peace and prosperity. Shown in the foreground is a ram of the *churro* breed common to all the missions. The coarse wool of these sheep was used to produce blankets and clothing for the neophytes.

**San Luis Rey de Francia, founded 1798.** Named for the crusading King Louis IX of France, this mission was known for its size, and not for its namesake, as the "King of the Missions." Its buildings covered more than six acres, with an elaborate water system and sunken gardens, while the cruciform church could hold a thousand worshippers.

**Santa Inés Virgen y Mártir, founded 1804.** Begun with the assistance of trained neophytes from neighboring missions, this was the last mission to be established in southern California. A great earthquake in 1812 brought down the church and damaged many other buildings. The present church was dedicated in 1817. Among the many artifacts left after the end of the mission era was a yellow silk parasol that had belonged to one of the padres.

**San Rafael Arcángel, founded 1817.** Though originally intended as a sanatorium for the ailing neophytes of Mission Dolores, San Rafael was granted full mission status in 1823. In the coming years, other missions in the area continued to send their ailing to San Rafael to recuperate. Among these were many children, for whom fresh milk was probably a necessity.

**San Francisco Solano, founded 1823.** The twenty-first and final mission in the California chain began as an attempt to transfer Mission San Francisco de Asís (Dolores) north of the bay, with the intention of abandoning the original, admittedly less hospitable, site. San Rafael was also to be transferred. In the end the plan failed; the two older missions continued while Solano was allowed to remain, partly as a buffer against the Russians, who had established settlements nearby. In 1846, the Bear Flag was raised in the adjacent plaza of Sonoma, marking the beginning of the American era.

# DOVER COLORING BOOKS

Paperbound unless otherwise indicated. Prices subject to change without notice. Available at your book dealer or write for free catalogues to Dept. 23, Dover Publications, Inc., 31 East 2nd Street, Mineola, N.Y. 11501. Please indicate field of interest. Each year Dover publishes over 200 books on fine art, music, crafts and needlework, antiques, languages, literature, children's books, chess, cookery, nature, anthropology, science, mathematics, and other areas.

*Manufactured in the U.S.A.*